# Keys

# to the

# Deeper Life

# KEYS
# TO THE
# DEEPER LIFE

by

A. W. TOZER

MOCKINGBIRD
PRESS

Copyright © 2022 Mockingbird Press

All rights reserved. The original works are in the public domain to the best of publisher's knowledge. The publisher makes no claim to the original writings. However, the compilation, construction, cover design, trademarks, derivations, foreword, descriptions, added work, etc., of this edition are copyrighted and may not be reproduced, distributed, or transmitted in any form or by any means, including photocopying, recording, or other electronic or mechanical methods, without the prior written permission of the publisher, except in the case of brief quotations embodied in critical reviews and certain other non-commercial uses permitted by copyright law, or where content is specifically noted as being reproduced under a Creative Commons license.

Cover, "Forest," by Christian Rohlfs, 1900
Foreword, Copyright © 2022 Mockingbird Press, LLC
Cover Design by Matthew Johnson, Copyright © 2021 Mockingbird Press, LLC
Interior Design by Daria Lacy

Publisher's Cataloging-In-Publication Data

Tozer, A.W., author; with Underhill, Rachael, Foreword by
Keys to the Deeper Life / A.W. Tozer; with Rachael Underhill

| | |
|---|---|
| Paperback | ISBN-13: 978-1-68493-009-8 |
| Hardback | ISBN-13: 978-1-68493-010-4 |
| Ebook | ISBN-13: 978-1-68493-011-1 |

1. Religion—Christian Living—General. 2. Philosophy & Religion—Religion & Be-liefs—Christianity—Christian Life & Practice, I. A.W. Tozer. II. Rachael Underhill. III. Keys to the Deeper Life.

REL012000 / QRMP

Type Set in Century Schoolbook / **Franklin Gothic Demi**

Mockingbird Press, Augusta, GA
info@mockingbirdpress.com

# Contents

Foreword .......................................................................... vii
No Revival Without Reformation .................................. 1
The Deeper Life: What is it? ........................................... 9
Gifts Of The Spirit: Are They For Us Today? ............ 19
How To Be Filled With The Spirit .............................. 27

# Foreword

Keys to the Deeper Life is a collection of theological essays written by American pastor and writer A.W. Tozer. Originally printed in Christian Life magazine, these essays ask the faithful to reject worldliness and instead return to "New Testament Christianity" where they will find a "deeper life" and greater connection to God.

A.W. Tozer (b. 1897, d. 1963) was called to Christianity as a teen. One day while walking home from his job at a tire factory, he reportedly heard a street preacher say, "If you don't know how to be saved ... just call on God, saying 'Lord be merciful to me a sinner.'" He did as the preacher said upon his return home.

Within five years, the self-educated youth became pastor of his first church. Although he did not get any formal education after sixth grade, he did receive honorary doctorates from Houghton and Wheaton. He spent his career as a pastor with the Christian and Missionary Alliance and began writing for Alliance Weekly magazine in 1931. By 1950, he was its editor.

Tozer and his wife had seven children and lived lives of giving and simplicity. They never owned a car, and

Tozer gave a great deal of his earnings from his twelve books and many more articles to the needy.

He was one of the most widely-read Christian authors of his time, which becomes understandable when one experiences his simple, layperson style of writing. He was also a powerful preacher. When asked by one of his mentees how he prepared a sermon, he replied that he simply prayed, and God showed him which scriptures his congregants needed to hear.

*Keys to the Deeper Life*, Tozer's 8th book published in 1957, is a short collection of essays to help contemporary Christians build a deeper spiritual connection with God and their faith. A common theme throughout his writing is the worldliness of modern Christians, at the expense of the "deeper riches of life."

The four essays in this work are:
*No Revival without Reformation*
*The Deeper Life, What Is It?*
*Gifts of the Spirit: Are They for Us Today?*
*How to Be Filled with the Spirit*

In *No Revival without Reformation*, Tozer argues that rather than seek a revival of the church by increasing its numbers, Christians must reform their lives first and give new obedience to God's commandments. He writes, "We must return to New Testament Christianity, not in creed only but in complete manner of life as well." And he did not leave himself out of this judgement: "And this applies to this writer and to this magazine as well as to everyone that names the name of Jesus."

*The Deeper Life, What Is It*, expresses concern about his contemporaries' satisfaction with an average spiritual existence, and instead exhorts the faithful to "explore the depths of the Christian evangel for those riches it surely contains but which we are as surely missing."

*In Gifts of the Spirit: Are They for Us Today*, Tozer states that there are so few Christians who "want to experience whatever God has for them within the context of sound New Testament faith" that they are easy to overlook. But there are still a few who will welcome these spiritual gifts (including faith, gifts of healing, prophecy, and distinguishing between spirits, among others). And only those who are blessed "by the Spirit through gifts He has Himself implanted in the souls of redeemed men" can do God's eternal work.

In his final essay, *How to Be Filled with the Spirit*, Tozer outlines the necessary path to fulfillment. First, one must be certain it is possible to be so filled. Then, he must desire to be. This is no simple desire. The person must enthusiastically renounce the control of their life and cede their personality and "self-sins" to the Spirit. Only when they surrender fully will they be prepared to be filled with the Spirit.

Tozer's reliance on prayer and scriptures to support his writing makes his work simple yet profound, and as relevant now as it was during his lifetime.

# NO REVIVAL WITHOUT REFORMATION

Wherever Christians meet these days one word is sure to be heard constantly repeated; that word is revival.

In sermon, song and prayer we are forever reminding the Lord and each other that what we must have to solve all our spiritual problems is a "mighty, old-time revival." The religious press, too, has largely gone over to the proposition that revival is the one great need of the hour, and anyone who is capable of preparing a brief for revival is sure to find many editors who will publish it.

So strongly is the breeze blowing for revival that scarcely anyone appears to have the discernment or the courage to turn around and lean into the wind, even though the truth may easily lie in that direction. Religion has its vogues very much as do philosophy, politics and women's fashions. Historically the major world religions have had their periods of decline and recovery, and those recoveries are bluntly called revivals by the annalists.

Let us not forget that in some lands Islam is now enjoying a revival, and the latest report from Japan indicates that after a brief eclipse following World War II Shintoism is making a remarkable come-back. In our own country Roman Catholicism as well as liberal Protestantism is moving forward at such a rate that the word revival is almost necessary to describe the phenomenon. And this without any perceptible elevation of the moral standards of its devotees.

A religion, even popular Christianity, could enjoy a boom altogether divorced from the transforming power of the Holy Spirit and so leave the church of the next generation worse off than it would have been if the boom had never occurred. I believe that the imperative need of the day is not simply revival, but a radical reformation that will go to the root of our moral and spiritual maladies and deal with causes rather than with consequences, with the disease rather than with symptoms.

It is my considered opinion that under the present circumstances we do not want revival at all. A widespread revival of the kind of Christianity we know today in America might prove to be a moral tragedy from which we would not recover in a hundred years.

Here are my reasons. A generation ago, as a reaction from Higher Criticism and its offspring, Modernism, there arose in Protestantism a powerful movement in defense of the historic Christian faith. This, for obvious reasons, came to be known as Fundamentalism. It was a more or less spontaneous movement without much organization, but its purpose wherever it appeared was the same: to stay "the rising tide of negation" in Christian theology and to restate and defend the basic doctrines of New Testament Christianity. This much is history.

## Falls Victim To Its Virtues

What is generally overlooked is that Fundamentalism, as it spread throughout the various denominations and non-denominational groups, fell victim to its own virtues. The Word died in the hands of its friends. Verbal inspiration, for instance (a doctrine which I have always held and do now hold), soon became afflicted with rigor mortis. The voice of the prophet was silenced and the scribe captured the minds of the faithful. In large areas the religious imagination withered. An unofficial hierarchy decided what Christians were to believe. Not the Scriptures, but what the scribe thought the Scriptures meant became the Christian creed. Christian colleges, seminaries, Bible institutes, Bible conferences, popular Bible expositors all joined to promote the cult of textualism. The system of extreme dispensationalism which was devised, relieved the Christian of repentance, obedience and cross-carrying in any other than the most formal sense. Whole sections of the New Testament were taken from the Church and disposed of after a rigid system of "dividing the Word of truth."

All this resulted in a religious mentality inimical to the true faith of Christ. A kind of cold mist settled over Fundamentalism. Below, the terrain was familiar. This was New Testament Christianity, to be sure. The basic doctrines of the Bible were there, but the climate was just not favorable to the sweet fruits of the Spirit.

The whole mood was different from that of the Early Church and of the great souls who suffered and sang and worshiped in the centuries past. The doctrines were sound but something vital was missing. The tree of correct doctrine was never allowed to blossom. The voice of the turtle [dove] was rarely heard in the land; instead, the parrot sat on his artificial perch and dutifully repeated what he had been taught and the whole emotional tone was somber and dull. Faith, a mighty, vitalizing doctrine in the mouths of the apostles, became in the mouth of the scribe another thing altogether and power went from it. As the letter triumphed, the Spirit withdrew and textualism ruled supreme. It was the time of the believer's Babylonian captivity.

In the interest of accuracy it should be said that this was a general condition only. Certainly there were some even in those low times whose longing hearts were better theologians than their teachers were. These pressed on to a fullness and power unknown to the rest. But they were not many and the odds were too great; they could not dispel the mist that hung over the land.

The error of textualism is not doctrinal. It is far more subtle than that and much more difficult to discover, but its effects are just as deadly. Not its theological beliefs are at fault, but its assumptions.

It assumes, for instance, that if we have the word for a thing we have the thing itself. If it is in the Bible, it is in us. If we have the doctrine, we have the experience. If something was true of Paul it is of necessity true of us because we accept Paul's epistles as divinely inspired. The Bible tells us how to be saved, but textualism goes on to make it tell us that we are saved, something which in the very nature of things it cannot do. Assurance of individual salvation is thus no more than a logical conclusion drawn from doctrinal premises, and the resultant experience wholly mental.

## Revolt From Mental Tyranny

Then came the revolt. The human mind can endure textualism just so long before it seeks a way of escape. So, quietly and quite unaware that any revolt was taking place, the masses of Fundamentalism reacted, not from the teaching of the Bible but from the mental tyranny of the scribes. With the recklessness of drowning men they fought their way up for air and struck out blindly for greater freedom of thought and for the emotional satisfaction their natures demanded and their teachers denied them.

The result over the last 20 years has been a religious debauch hardly equaled since Israel worshiped the golden calf. Of us Bible Christians it may truthfully be said that we "sat down to eat and to drink, and rose up to play." The separating line between the Church and the world has been all but obliterated.

Aside from a few of the grosser sins, the sins of the unregenerated world are now approved by a shocking number of professedly "born-again" Christians, and copied eagerly. Young Christians take as their models the rankest kind of worldlings and try to be as much like them as possible. Religious leaders have adopted the techniques of the advertisers; boasting, baiting and shameless exaggerating are now carried on as a normal procedure in church work. The moral climate is not that of the New Testament, but that of Hollywood and Broadway.

Most evangelicals no longer initiate; they imitate, and the world is their model. The holy faith of our fathers has in many places been made a form of entertainment, and the appalling thing is that all this has been fed down to the masses from the top.

That note of protest which began with the New Testament and which was always heard loudest when the Church was most powerful has been successfully silenced. The radical element in testimony and life that once made Christians hated by the world is missing from present-day evangelicalism. Christians were once revolutionists—moral, not political—but we have lost our revolutionary character. It is no longer either dangerous or costly to be a Christian. Grace has become not free, but cheap. We are busy these days proving to the world that they can have all the benefits of the Gospel without any inconvenience to their customary way of life. It's "all this, and heaven too."

This description of modern Christianity, while not universally applicable, is yet true of an overwhelming majority of present-day Christians. For this reason it is useless for large companies of believers to spend long hours begging God to send revival. Unless we intend to reform we may as well not pray. Unless praying men have the insight and faith to amend their whole way of life to conform to the New Testament pattern there can be no true revival.

## When Praying Is Wrong

Sometimes praying is not only useless, it is wrong. Here is an example: Israel had been defeated at Ai, and "Joshua rent his clothes, and fell to the earth upon his face before the ark of the Lord until the eventide, he and the elders of Israel, and put dust upon their heads."

According to our modern philosophy of revival this was the thing to do and, if continued long enough, should certainly have persuaded God and brought the blessing. But "the Lord said unto Joshua, Get thee up; wherefore liest thou upon thy face? Israel hath sinned, and they have also transgressed my covenant which I commanded them . . . Up, sanctify the people, and say, Sanctify yourselves against tomorrow; for thus saith the Lord God of Israel. There is an accursed thing in the midst of thee, O Israel: thou canst not stand before thine enemies, until ye take away the accursed thing from among you."

We must have a reformation within the Church. To beg for a flood of blessing to come upon a backslidden and disobedient Church is to waste time and effort. A new wave of religious interest will do no more than add numbers to churches that have no intention to own the Lordship of Jesus and come under obedience to His commandments. God is not interested in increased church attendance unless those who attend amend their ways and begin to live holy lives.

Once the Lord through the mouth of the prophet Isaiah said a word that should settle this thing forever: "To what purpose is the multitude of your sacrifices unto me? saith the Lord: I am full of the burnt-offerings of rams, and the fat of fed beasts; and I delight not in the blood of bullocks, or of lambs, or of he goats. When ye come to appear before me, who hath required this at your hand, to tread my courts? Bring no more vain oblations; incense is an abomination unto me; the new moons and sabbaths, the calling of assemblies, I cannot away with; it is iniquity, even the solemn meeting . . . Wash you, make you clean; put away the evil of your doings from before mine eyes; cease to do evil; learn to do well; seek judgment, relieve the oppressed, judge the fatherless, plead for the widow . . . If ye be willing and obedient, ye shall eat the good of the land."

Prayer for revival will prevail when it is accompanied by radical amendment of life; not before. All-night prayer meetings that are not preceded by practical repentance may actually be displeasing to God. "To obey is better than sacrifice."

We must return to New Testament Christianity, not in creed only but in complete manner of life as well. Separation, obedience, humility, simplicity, gravity, self-control, modesty, cross-bearing: these all must again be made a living part of the total Christian concept and be carried out in everyday conduct. We must cleanse the temple of the hucksters and the money changers and come fully under the authority of our risen Lord once more. And this applies to this writer and to this magazine as well as to everyone that names the name of Jesus. Then we can pray with confidence and expect true revival to follow.

# THE DEEPER LIFE: WHAT IS IT?

Suppose some angelic being who had since creation known the deep, still rapture of dwelling in the divine Presence would appear on earth and live awhile among us Christians. Don't you imagine he might be astonished at what he saw?

He might, for instance, wonder how we can be contented with our poor, commonplace level of spiritual experience. In our hands, after all, is a message from God not only inviting us into His holy fellowship but also giving us detailed instructions about how to get there. After feasting on the bliss of intimate communion with God how could such a being understand the casual, easily satisfied spirit which characterizes most evangelicals today? And if our hypothetical being knew such blazing souls as Moses, David, Isaiah, Paul, John, Stephen, Augustine, Rolle, Rutherford, Newton, Brainerd and Faber, he might logically conclude that 20th century Christians had misunderstood some vital doctrine of the faith somewhere and had stopped short of a true acquaintance with God.

What if he sat in on the daily sessions of an average Bible conference and noted the extravagant claims, we

Christians make for ourselves as believers in Christ and compared them with our actual spiritual experiences? He would surely conclude that there was a serious contradiction between what we think we are and what we are in reality. The bold claims that we are sons of God, that we are risen with Christ and seated with Him in heavenly places, that we are indwelt by the life-giving Spirit, that we are members of the Body of Christ and children of the new creation, are negated by our attitudes, our behavior and, most of all, by our lack of fervor and by the absence of a spirit of worship within us.

Perhaps if our heavenly visitor pointed out the great disparity between our doctrinal beliefs and our lives, he might be dismissed with a smiling explanation that it is but the normal difference between our sure standing and our variable state. Certainly then, he would be appalled that as beings once made in the image of God we could allow ourselves thus to play with words and trifle with our own souls.

Significant, isn't it, that of all who hold the evangelical position those Christians who lay the greatest store by Paul are often the least Pauline in spirit. There is a vast and important difference between a Pauline creed and a Pauline life. Some of us who have for years sympathetically observed the Christian scene feel constrained to paraphrase the words of the dying queen and cry out, "O Paul! Paul! what evils have been committed in thy name." Tens of thousands of believers who pride themselves on their understanding of Romans and Ephesians cannot conceal the sharp spiritual contradiction that exists between their hearts and the heart of Paul.

That difference may be stated this way: Paul was a seeker and a finder and a seeker still. They seek and find and seek no more. After "accepting" Christ they tend to substitute logic for life and doctrine for experience.

For them the truth becomes a veil to hide the face of God; for Paul it was a door into His very Presence. Paul's spirit was that of the loving explorer. He was a prospector among the hills of God searching for the gold of personal spiritual acquaintance. Many today stand by Paul's doctrine who will not follow him in his passionate yearning for divine reality. Can these be said to be Pauline in any but the most nominal sense?

## If Paul Were Preaching Today

With the words "That I may know him" Paul answered the whining claims of the flesh and raced on toward perfection. All gain he counted loss for the excellency of the knowledge of Christ Jesus the Lord, and if to know Him better meant suffering or even death it was all one to Paul. To him conformity to Christ was cheap at any price. He panted after God as the heart pants after the waterbrook, and calm reason had little to do with the way he felt.

Indeed a score of cautious and ignoble excuses might have been advanced to slow him down, and we have heard them all. "Watch out for your health," a prudent friend warns. "There is danger that you become mentally unbalanced," says another. "You'll get a reputation for being an extremist," cries a third, and a sober Bible teacher with more theology than thirst hurries to assure him that there is nothing more to seek. "You are accepted in the beloved," he says, "and blessed with all spiritual blessings in heavenly places in Christ. What more do you want? You have only to believe and to wait for the day of His triumph."

So Paul would be exhorted if he lived among us today, for so in substance have I heard the holy aspirations of the saints damped down and smothered as they leaped up to meet God in an increasing degree of intimacy. But knowing Paul as we do, it is safe to assume that he would ignore this low counsel of expediency and press onward toward the mark for the prize of the high calling of God in Christ Jesus. And we do well to follow him.

When the apostle cries "That I may know him," he uses the word know not in its intellectual but in its experiential sense. We must look for the meaning—not to the mind but to the heart. Theological knowledge is knowledge about God. While this is indispensable it is not sufficient. It bears the same relation to man's spiritual need as a well does to the need of his physical body. It is not the rock-lined pit for which the dusty traveler longs, but the sweet, cool water that flows up from it. It is not intellectual knowledge about God that quenches man's ancient heart-thirst, but the very Person and Presence of God Himself. These come to us through Christian doctrine, but they are more than doctrine.

Christian truth is designed to lead us to God, not to serve as a substitute for God.

## A New Yearning Among Evangelicals

Within the hearts of a growing number of evangelicals in recent days has arisen a new yearning after an above-average spiritual experience. Yet the greater number still shy away from it and raise objections that evidence misunderstanding or fear or plain unbelief. They point to the neurotic, the psychotic, the pseudo-Christian cultist and the intemperate fanatic, and lump them all together without discrimination as followers of the "deeper life."

While this is of course completely preposterous, the fact that such confusion exists obliges those who advocate the Spirit-filled life to define their terms and explain their position. Just what, then, do we mean? And what are we advocating?

For myself, I am reverently concerned that I teach nothing but Christ crucified. For me to accept a teaching or even an emphasis, I must be persuaded that it is scriptural and altogether apostolic in spirit and temper. And it must be in full harmony with the best in the historic church and in the tradition marked by the finest devotional works, the sweetest and most radiant hymnody and the loftiest experiences revealed in Christian biography.

It must lie within the pattern of truth that gave us such saintly souls as Bernard of Clairvaux, John of the

Cross, Molinos, Nicholas of Cusa, John Fletcher, David Brainerd, Reginald Heber, Evan Roberts, General Booth and a host of other like souls who, while they were less gifted and lesser known, constitute what Dr. Paul S. Rees (in another context) calls "the seed of survival." And his term is apt, for it was such extraordinary Christians as these who saved Christianity from collapsing under the sheer weight of the spiritual mediocrity it was compelled to carry.

To speak of the "deeper life" is not to speak of anything deeper than simple New Testament religion. Rather it is to insist that believers explore the depths of the Christian evangel for those riches it surely contains but which we are as surely missing. The "deeper life" is deeper only because the average Christian life is tragically shallow.

They who advocate the deeper life today might compare unfavorably with almost any of the Christians that surrounded Paul or Peter in early times. While they may not as yet have made much progress, their faces are toward the light and they are beckoning us on. It is hard to see how we can justify our refusal to heed their call.

What the deeper life advocates are telling us is that we should press on to enjoy in personal inward experience the exalted privileges that are ours in Christ Jesus; that we should insist upon tasting the sweetness of internal worship in spirit as well as in truth; that to reach this ideal we should if necessary push beyond our contented brethren and bring upon ourselves whatever opposition may follow as a result.

The author of the celebrated devotional work, The Cloud of Unknowing, begins his little book with a prayer that expresses the spirit of the deeper life teaching: "God, unto whom all hearts be open . . . and unto whom no secret thing is hid, I beseech Thee so for to cleanse the intent of mine heart with the unspeakable gift of Thy grace, that I may perfectly love Thee and worthily praise Thee. Amen."

Who that is truly born of the Spirit, unless he has been prejudiced by wrong teaching, can object to such a thorough cleansing of the heart as will enable him perfectly to love God and worthily to praise Him? Yet this is exactly what we mean when we speak about the "deeper life" experience. Only we mean that it should be literally fulfilled within the heart, not merely accepted by the head.

Nicephorus, a father of the Eastern Church, in a little treatise on the Spirit-filled life, begins with a call that sounds strange to us only because we have been for so long accustomed to following Jesus afar off and to living among a people that follow Him afar off. "You, who desire to capture the wondrous divine illumination of our Savior Jesus Christ—who seek to feel the divine fire in your heart—who strive to sense and experience the feeling of reconciliation with God—who, in order to unearth the treasure buried in the field of your heart and to gain possession of it, have renounced everything worldly—who desire the candles of your souls to burn brightly even now, and who for this purpose have renounced all the world—who wish by conscious experience to know and to receive the kingdom of heaven existing within you—come and I will impart to you the science of eternal heavenly life—"

Such quotations as these might easily be multiplied till they filled half a dozen volumes. This yearning after God has never completely died in any generation. Always there were some who scorned the low paths and insisted upon walking the high road of spiritual perfection. Yet, strangely enough, that word perfection never meant a spiritual terminal point nor a state of purity that made watchfulness and prayer unnecessary. Exactly the opposite was true.

## Hearing But Not Obeying

It has been the unanimous testimony of the greatest Christian souls that the nearer they drew to God the more acute became their consciousness of sin and their sense of personal unworthiness. The purest souls never knew how pure they were and the greatest saints never guessed that they were great. The very thought that they were good or great would have been rejected by them as a temptation of the devil.

They were so engrossed with gazing upon the face of God that they spent scarce a moment looking at themselves. They were suspended in that sweet paradox of spiritual awareness where they knew that they were clean through the blood of the Lamb and yet felt that they deserved only death and hell as their just reward. This feeling is strong in the writings of Paul and is found also in almost all devotional books and among the greatest and most loved hymns.

The quality of evangelical Christianity must be greatly improved if the present unusual interest in religion is not to leave the church worse off than she was before the phenomenon emerged. If we listen I believe we will hear the Lord say to us what He once said to Joshua, "Arise, go over this Jordan, thou, and all this people, unto the and which I do give to them, even to the children of Israel." Or we will hear the writer to the Hebrews say, "Therefore, leaving the first principles of the doctrine of Christ, let us go on unto perfection." And surely we will hear Paul exhort us to "be filled with the Spirit."

If we are alert enough to hear God's voice we must not content ourselves with merely "believing" it. How can any man believe a command? Commands are to be obeyed, and until we have obeyed them we have done exactly nothing at all about them. And to have heard them and not obeyed them is infinitely worse than never to have heard them at all, especially in the light of Christ's soon return and the judgment to come.

# GIFTS OF THE SPIRIT: ARE THEY FOR US TODAY?

"Concerning spiritual gifts, brethren," wrote Paul to the Corinthians, "I would not have you ignorant."

Certainly, Paul meant nothing derogatory by this. Rather, he was expressing a charitable concern that his fellow believers should be neither uninformed nor in error about a truth so vastly important as this one.

For some time, it has been evident that we evangelicals have been failing to avail ourselves of the deeper riches of grace that lie in the purposes of God for us. As a consequence, we have been suffering greatly, even tragically. One blessed treasure we have missed is the right to possess the gifts of the Spirit as set forth in such fullness and clarity in the New Testament.

Before proceeding further, however, I want to make it plain that I have had no change of mind about the matter. What I write here has been my faith for many years. No recent spiritual experience has altered my beliefs in any way. I merely bring together truths which I have held during my entire public ministry and have preached with a fair degree of consistency where and when I felt my hearers could receive them.

In their attitude toward the gifts of the Spirit Christians over the last few years have tended to divide themselves into three groups.

First, there are those who magnify the gifts of the Spirit until they can see little else.

Second, there are those who deny that the gifts of the Spirit are intended for the Church in this period of her history.

Third, there are those who appear to be thoroughly bored with the whole thing and do not care to discuss it.

More recently we have become aware of another group, so few in number as scarcely to call for classification. It consists of those who want to know the truth about the Spirit's gifts and to experience whatever God has for them within the context of sound New Testament faith. It is for these that this is written.

## What Is The True Church?

Every spiritual problem is at bottom theological. Its solution will depend upon the teaching of the Holy Scriptures plus a correct understanding of that teaching. That correct understanding constitutes a spiritual philosophy, that is, a viewpoint, a high vantage ground from which the whole landscape may be seen at once, each detail appearing in its proper relation to everything else. Once such vantage ground is gained, we are in a position to evaluate any teaching or interpretation that is offered us in the name of truth.

A proper understanding of the gifts of the Spirit in the Church must depend upon a right concept of the nature of the Church. The gift problem cannot be isolated from the larger question and settled by itself.

The true Church is a spiritual phenomenon appearing in human society and intermingling with it to some degree but differing from it sharply in certain vital characteristics. It is composed of regenerated persons who differ from other human beings in that they have a superior kind of life imparted to them at the time of their inward renewal.

They are children of God in a sense not true of any other created beings.

Their origin is divine and their citizenship is in heaven.

They worship God in the Spirit, rejoice in Jesus Christ and have no confidence in the flesh.

They constitute a chosen generation, a royal priesthood, a holy nation, a peculiar people.

They have espoused the cause of a rejected and crucified Man Who claimed to be God and Who has pledged His sacred honor that He will prepare a place for them in His Father's house and return again to conduct them there with rejoicing.

In the meantime they carry His cross, suffer whatever indignities men may heap upon them for His sake, act as His ambassadors and do good to all men in His name.

They steadfastly believe that they will share His triumph, and for this reason they are perfectly willing to share His rejection by a society that does not understand them.

And they have no hard feelings—only charity and compassion and a strong desire that all men may come to repentance and be reconciled to God.

This is a fair summary of one aspect of New Testament teaching about the Church. But another truth more revealing and significant to those seeking information about the gifts of the Spirit is that the Church is a spiritual body, an organic entity united by the life that dwells within it.

## Each Member Joined Together

Each member is joined to the whole by a relationship of life. As a man's soul may be said to be the life of his body, so the indwelling Spirit is the life of the Church.

The idea that the Church is the body of Christ is not an erroneous one, resulting from the pressing too far of a mere figure of speech. The apostle Paul in three of his epistles sets forth this truth in such sobriety of tone and fullness of detail as to preclude the notion that he is employing a casual figure of speech not intended to be taken too literally.

The clear, emphatic teaching of the great apostle is that Christ is the Head of the Church which is His body. The parallel is drawn carefully and continued through long passages. Conclusions are drawn from the doctrine and certain moral conduct is made to depend upon it.

As a normal man consists of a body with various obedient members with a head to direct them, so the true Church is a body, individual Christians being the members and Christ the Head.

The mind works through the members of the body, using them to fulfill its intelligent purposes. Paul speaks of the foot, the hand, the ear, the eye as being members of the body, each with its proper but limited function; but it is the Spirit the worketh in them (I Cor. 12:1-31).

The teaching that the Church is the body of Christ in I Corinthians 12 follows a listing of certain spiritual gifts and reveals the necessity for those gifts.

The intelligent head can work only as it has at its command organs designed for various tasks. It is the mind that sees, but it must have an eye to see through. It is the mind that hears, but it cannot hear without an ear.

And so with all the varied members which are the instruments by means of which the mind moves into the external world to carry out its plans.

As all man's work is done by his mind, so the work of the Church is done by the Spirit, and by Him alone. But to work He must set in the body certain members with abilities specifically created to act as media through which the Spirit can flow toward ordained ends. That in brief is the philosophy of the gifts of the Spirit.

## How Many Gifts?

It is usually said that there are nine gifts of the Spirit. (I suppose because Paul lists nine in I Corinthians 12.) Actually, Paul mentions no less than 17 (I Cor. 12:4-11, 27-31; Rom. 12:3-8; Eph. 4:7-11). And these are not natural talents merely, but gifts imparted by the Holy Spirit to fit the believer for his place in the body of Christ. They are like pipes on a great organ, permitting the musician wide scope and range to produce music of the finest quality. But they are, I repeat, more than talents. They are spiritual gifts.

Natural talents enable a man to work within the field of nature; but through the body of Christ God is doing an eternal work above and beyond the realm of fallen nature. This requires supernatural working.

Religious work can be done by natural men without the gifts of the Spirit, and it can be done well and skillfully. But work designed for eternity can only be done by the eternal Spirit. No work has eternity in it unless it is done by the Spirit through gifts He has Himself implanted in the souls of redeemed men.

For a generation certain evangelical teachers have told us that the gifts of the Spirit ceased at the death of the apostles or at the completion of the New Testament. This, of course, is a doctrine without a syllable of biblical authority back of it. Its advocates must accept full responsibility for thus manipulating the Word of God.

The result of this erroneous teaching is that spiritually gifted persons are ominously few among us. When we so desperately need leaders with the gift of discernment, for instance, we do not have them and are compelled to fall back upon the techniques of the world.

This frightening hour calls aloud for men with the gift of prophetic insight. Instead we have men who conduct surveys, polls and panel discussions.

We need men with the gift of knowledge. In their place we have men with scholarship—nothing more.

Thus we may be preparing ourselves for the tragic hour when God may set us aside as so-called evangelicals and raise up another movement to keep New Testament Christianity alive in the earth. Say not, "We be children of Abraham. God is able of these stones to raise up children unto Abraham."

The truth of the matter is that the Scriptures plainly imply the imperative of possessing the gifts of the Spirit. Paul urges that we both "covet" and "desire" spiritual gifts (I Cor. 12:31, I Cor. 14:1). It does not appear to be an optional matter with us but rather a scriptural mandate to those who have been filled with the Spirit.

But I must also add a word of caution.

The various spiritual gifts are not equally valuable, as Paul so carefully explained.

Certain brethren have magnified one gift out of 17 out of all proportion. Among these brethren there have been and are many godly souls, but the general moral results of this teaching have nevertheless not been good.

In practice it has resulted in much shameless exhibitionism, a tendency to depend upon experiences instead of upon Christ and often a lack of ability to distinguish the works of the flesh from the operations of the Spirit.

Those who deny that the gifts are for us today and those who insist upon making a hobby of one gift are both wrong, and we are all suffering the consequence of their error.

Today there is no reason for our remaining longer in doubt. We have every right to expect our Lord to grant to His Church the spiritual gifts which He has never in fact taken away from us, but which we are failing to receive only because of our error or unbelief.

It is more than possible that God is even now imparting the gifts of the Spirit to whomsoever He can and in whatever measure He can as His conditions are met even imperfectly. Otherwise the torch of truth would flicker out and die.

Clearly, however, we have yet to see what God would do for His Church if we would all throw ourselves down before Him with an open Bible and cry, "Behold Thy servant, Lord! Be it unto me even as Thou wilt."

# How To Be Filled With The Spirit

Almost all Christians want to be full of the Spirit. Only a few want to be filled with the Spirit.

But how can a Christian know the fullness of the Spirit unless he has known the experience of being filled?

It would, however, be useless to tell anyone how to be filled with the Spirit unless he first believes that he can be. No one can hope for something he is not convinced is the will of God for him and within the bounds of scriptural provision.

Before the question "How can I be filled?" has any validity the seeker after God must be sure that the experience of being filled is actually possible. The man who is not sure can have no ground of expectation. Where there is no expectation there can be no faith, and where there is no faith the inquiry is meaningless.

The doctrine of the Spirit as it relates to the believer has over the last half century been shrouded in a mist such as lies upon a mountain in stormy weather. A world of confusion has surrounded this truth. The children of God have been taught contrary doctrines from the same texts, warned, threatened and intimidated until they instinctively recoil from every mention of the Bible teaching concerning the Holy Spirit.

This confusion has not come by accident. An enemy has done this. Satan knows that Spiritless evangelicalism is as deadly as Modernism or heresy, and he has done everything in his power to prevent us from enjoying our true Christian heritage.

A church without the Spirit is as helpless as Israel might have been in the wilderness if the fiery cloud had deserted them. The Holy Spirit is our cloud by day and our fire by night. Without Him we only wander aimlessly about the dessert.

That is what we today are surely doing. We have divided ourselves into little ragged groups, each one running after a will-o'-the-wisp or firefly in the mistaken notion that we are following the Shekinah. It is not only desirable that the cloudy pillar should begin to glow again. It is imperative.

The Church can have light only as it is full of the Spirit, and it can be full only as the members that compose it are filled individually. Furthermore, no one can be filled until he is convinced that being filled is a part of the total plan of God in redemption; that it is nothing added or extra, nothing strange or queer, but a proper and spiritual operation of God, based upon and growing out of the work of Christ in atonement.

The inquirer must be sure to the point of conviction. He must believe that the whole thing is normal and right. He must believe that God wills that he be anointed with a horn of fresh oil beyond and in addition to all the ten thousand blessings he may already have received from the good hand of God.

Until he is so convinced I recommend that he take time out to fast and pray and meditate upon the Scriptures. Faith comes from the Word of God. Suggestion, exhortation or the psychological effect of the testimony of others who may have been filled will not suffice.

Unless he is persuaded from the Scriptures, he should not press the matter nor allow himself to fall victim to the emotional manipulators intent upon forcing the issue. God is wonderfully patient and understanding and will wait for the slow heart to catch up with the truth. In the meantime, the seeker should be calm and confident. In due time God will lead him through the Jordan. Let him not break loose and run ahead. Too many have done so, only to bring disaster upon their Christian lives.

After a man is convinced that he can be filled with the Spirit he must desire to be. To the interested inquirer I ask these questions: Are you sure that you want to be possessed by a Spirit Who, while He is pure and gentle and wise and loving, will yet insist upon being Lord of your life? Are you sure you want your personality to be taken over by One Who will require obedience to the written Word? Who will not tolerate any of the self-sins in your life: self-love, self-indulgence? Who will not permit you to strut or boast or show off? Who will take the direction of your life away from you and will reserve the sovereign right to test you and discipline you? Who will strip away from you many loved objects which secretly harm your soul?

Unless you can answer an eager "Yes" to these questions you do not want to be filled. You may want the thrill or the victory or the power, but you do not really want to be filled with the Spirit. Your desire is little more than a feeble wish and is not pure enough to please God, Who demands all or nothing.

Again I ask: Are you sure you need to be filled with the Spirit? Tens of thousands of Christians, laymen, preachers, missionaries, manage to get on somehow without having had a clear experience of being filled. That Spiritless labor can lead only to tragedy in the day of Christ is something the average Christian seems to have forgotten. But how about you?

Perhaps your doctrinal bias is away from belief in the crisis of the Spirit's filling. Very well, look at the fruit of such doctrine. What is your life producing? You are doing religious work, preaching, singing, writing, promoting, but what is the quality of your work? True; you received the Spirit at the moment of conversion, but is it also true that you are ready without a further anointing to resist temptation, obey the Scriptures, understand the truth, live victoriously, die in peace and meet Christ without embarrassment at His coming?

If, on the other hand, your soul cries out for God, for the living God, and your dry and empty heart despairs of living a normal Christian life without a further anointing, then I ask you: Is your desire all-absorbing? Is it the biggest thing in your life? Does it crowd out every common religious activity and fill you with an acute longing that can only be described as the pain of desire? If your heart cries "Yes" to these questions you may be on your way to a spiritual breakthrough that will transform your whole life.

It is in the preparation for receiving the Spirit's anointing that most Christians fail. Probably no one was ever filled without first having gone through a period of deep soul disturbance and inward turmoil. When we find ourselves entering this state the temptation is to panic and draw back. Satan exhorts us to take it easy lest we make shipwreck of the faith, and dishonor the Lord that bought us.

Of course, he cares nothing for us nor for our Lord. His purpose is to keep us weak and unarmed in a day of conflict. And millions of believers accept his hypocritical lies as gospel truth and go back to their caves like the prophets of Obadiah to feed on bread and water.

Before there can be fullness there must be emptiness. Before God can fill us with Himself, we must first be emptied of ourselves. It is this emptying that brings the painful disappointment and despair of self of which so many persons have complained just prior to their new and radiant experience.

There must come a total of self-disvaluation, a death to all things without us and within us, or there can never be a real filling with the Holy Spirit.

*The dearest idol I have known,*
*Whate'er that idol be,*
*Help me to tear it from Thy throne,*
*And worship only Thee.*

We sing this glibly enough, but we cancel out our prayer by our refusal to surrender the very idol of which we sing. To give up our last idol is to plunge ourselves into a state of inward loneliness which no gospel meeting, no fellowship with other Christians, can ever cure. For this reason, most Christians play it safe and settle for a life of compromise.

They have some of God, to be sure, but not all; and God has some of them, but not all. And so, they live their tepid lives and try to disguise with bright smiles and snappy choruses the deep spiritual destitution within them.

One thing should be made crystal clear: The soul's journey through the dark night is not a meritorious one. The suffering and the loneliness do not make a man dear to God nor earn the horn of oil for which he yearns. We cannot buy anything from God. Everything comes out of His goodness on the grounds of Christ's redeeming blood and is a free gift, with no strings attached.

What the soul agony does is to break up the fallow ground, empty the vessel, detach the heart from earthly interests and focus the attention upon God.

All that has gone before is by way of soul preparation for the divine act of infilling. The infilling itself is not a complicated thing. While I shy away from "how to" formulas in spiritual things, I believe the answer to the question "How can I be filled?" may be answered in four words, all of them active verbs. They are these: (1) surrender, (2) ask, (3) obey, (4) believe.

Surrender: "I beseech you therefore, brethren, by the mercies of God, that ye present your bodies a living sacrifice, holy, acceptable unto God, which is your reasonable service. And be not conformed to this world: but be ye transformed by the renewing of your mind, that ye may prove what is that good, and acceptable, and perfect, will of God" (Rom. 12:1,2).

Ask: "If ye then, being evil, know how to give good gifts unto your children: how much more shall your heavenly Father give the Holy Spirit to them that ask him?" (Luke 11:13).

Obey: "We are his witnesses of these things; and so is also the Holy Ghost, whom God hath given to them that obey him" (Acts 5:32).

Complete and ungrudging obedience to the will of God is absolutely indispensable to the reception of the Spirit's anointing. As we wait before God we should reverently search the Scriptures and listen for the voice of gentle stillness to learn what our Heavenly Father expects of us. Then, trusting to His enabling, we should obey to the best of our ability and understanding.

Believe: This only would I learn of you, Received ye the Spirit by the works of the law, or by the hearing of faith?" (Gal. 3:2).

While the infilling of the Spirit is received by faith and only by faith, let us beware of that imitation faith which is no more than a mental assent to truth. It has been a source of great disappointment to multitudes of seeking souls. True faith invariably brings a witness.

But what is that witness? It is nothing physical, vocal nor psychical. The Spirit never commits Himself to the flesh. The only witness He gives is a subjective one, known to the individual alone. The Spirit announces

Himself to the deep-in spirit of the man. The flesh profiteth nothing, but the believing heart knows. Holy, holy, holy.

One last thing: Neither in the Old Testament nor in the New, nor in Christian testimony as found in the writings of the saints as far as my knowledge goes, was any believer ever filled with the Holy Spirit who did not know he had been filled. Neither was anyone filled who did not know when he was filled. And no one was ever filled gradually.

Behind these three trees many half-hearted souls have tried to hide like Adam from the presence of the Lord, but they are not good enough hiding places. The man who does not know when he was filled was never filled (though of course it is possible to forget the date). And the man who hopes to be filled gradually will never be filled at all.

In my sober judgment the relation of the Spirit to the believer is the most vital question the church faces today. The problems raised by Christian existentialism or neo-orthodoxy are nothing by comparison with this most critical one. Ecumenicity, eschatological theories—none of these things deserve consideration until every believer can give an affirmative answer to the question, "Have ye received the Holy Ghost since ye believed?"

And it might easily be that after we have been filled with the Spirit we will find to our delight that the very filling itself has solved the other problems for us.

www.ingramcontent.com/pod-product-compliance
Lightning Source LLC
Chambersburg PA
CBHW060345080526
44583CB00014B/1070